I accept all of my imperfections.

I am capable

Everything is possible.

I deserve to take up space.

Faith is sight unseen.

I am balanced.

I am kind to myself.

I am allowed to say no to what interrupts my peace.

I am worthy, I am enough.

I am grateful for the person that I am and excited for the person I am becoming.

I appreciate all the ways that I am unique.

I love my sisterhood that so have created around me.

I release tension whenever I exhale.

I am more than my negative thoughts.

I am intelligent and fun, and people enjoy talking to me.

I deserve to prioritize myself over anything else.

I take care of my body outwardly and inwardly.

I believe in building valuable relationships.

I understand that everyone is not like me, and that is okay.

I take pride in my appearance.

I use healthy methods to release my stress.

I cherish my crown and take care of it.

I appreciate time spent with my family and friends.

I receive all good things that come to me.

Abundance flows to me.

I take time to do things I enjoy.

Self care is important to me.

I'm mindful what I put into my body.

Creativity flows through me.

I am intentional of who I allow in my space.

Made in the USA
Columbia, SC
06 January 2025